# IMAGES OF WAR
# GERMAN ARMOUR LOST ON THE WESTERN FRONT

## RARE PHOTOGRAPHS FROM WARTIME ARCHIVES

# IMAGES OF WAR
# GERMAN ARMOUR LOST ON THE WESTERN FRONT

## RARE PHOTOGRAPHS FROM WARTIME ARCHIVES

## BOB CARRUTHERS

Pen & Sword
**MILITARY**

This edition published in 2018 by

Pen & Sword Military
An imprint of
Pen & Sword Books Ltd.
47 Church Street
Barnsley
South Yorkshire
S70 2AS

Copyright © Coda Publishing Ltd. 2018.
Published under licence by Pen & Sword Books Ltd.

ISBN: 9781473868526

Printed and bound in England
By CPI Group (UK) Ltd., Croydon, CR0 4YY

Pen & Sword Books Ltd. incorporates the imprints of Pen & Sword Aviation, Pen & Sword Family History, Pen & Sword Maritime, Pen & Sword Military, Pen & Sword Discovery, Pen & Sword Politics, Pen & Sword Atlas, Pen & Sword Archaeology, Wharncliffe Local History, Wharncliffe True Crime, Wharncliffe Transport, Pen & Sword Select, Pen & Sword Military Classics, Leo Cooper, The Praetorian Press, Claymore Press, Remember When, Seaforth Publishing and Frontline Publishing

For a complete list of Pen & Sword titles please contact

PEN & SWORD BOOKS LIMITED
47 Church Street, Barnsley, South Yorkshire, S70 2AS, England
E-mail: enquiries@pen-and-sword.co.uk
Website: www.pen-and-sword.co.uk

# INTRODUCTION

In April 1938, to mark the Führer's birthday, Hitler's magnificent new army marched before him. The event was designed to intimidate the world. At the centre of the great parade were the tanks of the new German Panzer Divisions. It is true that most of the tanks were small and lightly armed but the sheer numbers added to the aura of cutting edge military might.

Hitler was a gambler and he gambled upon bluffing his enemies into believing his tank forces were far stronger than they actually were. Out of sight of the foreign dignitaries, many vehicles re-joined the tail of the columns and were driven past twice. The trick worked and served Hitler's grand design. By a combination of deceit and brinkmanship Hitler had made a chilling and spectacular assertion of Germany's re-born military might.

Ironically, the roots of the German *Panzerwaffe* were laid in conjunction with Soviet Russia, the nation that was destined to become Nazi Germany's greatest enemy and ultimately her nemesis. During the 1920s, the new Soviet Union was an even greater pariah than Germany. Somehow the fledgling Soviet state had already withstood the perils of a civil war and foreign intervention, which had seen British ground troops deployed in an attempt to assist the White Russians. Clearly Moscow could not look to London or Paris for aid, so she turned instead to her former adversary. German/ Soviet tank development began at Kazan, located deep inside Russia where secrecy was relatively easy to maintain. The fruits of those clandestine operations were to be seen in action as the Soviet and German tank forces of 1941 locked horns in earnest.

As a result of General Heinz Guderian's efforts, in 1935, the first Panzer Divisions were formed. These revolutionary formations incorporated a tank brigade with 561 tanks providing the main firepower. A great deal of accurate thought had gone into the development of the Panzer Division, which also included motorised infantry, reconnaissance and artillery. The resulting Panzer Division was a well-balanced force that could call on the support of any or all of the component parts to capture an objective. The purpose of the Panzer Division was to launch a speedy advance, break through into enemy territory and spread confusion, fear, and panic in the enemy command and communication systems. One further innovation was the close link with the Luftwaffe, who could add even more firepower when needed.

Although comparatively few in number the mechanised and armoured units of the Second World War were the only truly modern component of the German Army and were the key to much of its extraordinary success. The military of many countries were familiar with wireless technology, with tanks and with war planes, but only in Germany were these elements so effectively combined to form fully integrated fighting units with exceptional striking power. The term blitzkrieg had first appeared in 1935, in a German

Heinz Guderian.

military periodical *Deutsche Wehr* (German Defence), in reference to sudden assaults that characterised the new combined arms tactics. The new breed of German tactics were successful in the campaigns of 1939-1941 and by 1940, the term blitzkrieg was being extensively used in the Western media.

It is difficult now to imagine that such small and lightly armoured tanks could spearhead the devastating operation of blitzkrieg. The secret of their success was speed and co-ordination of effort. In reality, the remarkable string of German successes was due less to superiority of military technology than to the excellence of German methods and training. Many of the early German Panzer Division were equipped only with Panzer I and II light tanks. It was the new way of waging war, which came as a hammer blow to Germany's opponents forcing them to radically rethink their own military tactics.

Hitler's Generals had certainly rewritten the rule book of battle. In Poland, it took less than a month to dispose of a large but poorly equipped Polish army that had fought along rigidly traditional lines. In France, the German army successfully challenged the largest and most modern army in Europe.

Only a year later, in June 1941, even this achievement was to be eclipsed by Germany's astonishing victories in the war against Stalin's Soviet Union. Spearheaded by tank formations, German armies swept eastward. In a series of huge encirclements, thousands of Soviet tanks were destroyed and millions of Soviet troops killed or captured, and for a while it seemed that Hitler would succeed where Napoleon had failed, by conquering the vast eastern power. On the world stage the tank had now become established as a symbol of German invincibility.

In the campaigns of the early war years these new tank armies struck down all before them, although a surprisingly large number of German tanks were knocked out in Poland and in France. However, it is always the case that history is recorded by the victor, and accordingly there are precious few shots of knocked out German armour from 1939-1941. Most of the photographs in these pages are therefore from the later stages of the war when allied reporters were on hand to record the victorious efforts of their kinsmen.

Tanks came of age in the Second World War. They also developed faster and changed more in a six-year period than at any time before or since. The catalyst was the demands of a technological war. Like a crazed version of Darwin's Theory of Evolution, the Second World War accelerated the pace of design. Fast responses to a constantly changing situation were urgently needed and new designs had to be engineered, tested, and built in an incredibly short timescale. In the space of three short years, German tank technology progressed from the lightweight and inefficient Panzer I to the mighty Tiger II (*Panzerkampfwagen* Tiger Ausf. B) – known to the allies as the 'King Tiger' or 'Royal Tiger'. This was one of the most feared fighting vehicles of the war, and an almost unbelievable leap in terms of design from the humble Panzer I.

The Tiger II heavy tank.

When attacking, explosive power alone had little value against the thick armour of a tank like the Tiger II. To destroy a tank, it was obviously necessary to fire a projectile fast enough to penetrate the armour of the hull and disable the machine, or kill the men inside. This required tanks to be able to fire the heaviest practicable shell, at huge speeds. This velocity produced enough kinetic force to punch through the armour of an enemy tank. Even today, armour-piercing rounds still tend to be solid shot rounds that rely upon a very high velocity. The enormous pressures created by a round impacting on armour force a way through the target and fly around inside destroying equipment, or killing or injuring the crew.

The armour of most tanks of 1939 and 1940 vintage could be penetrated by relatively small calibre anti-tank weapons, however, as armour grew in thickness a variety of high explosive anti-tank rounds had to be developed. These High Explosive Anti-Tank (HEAT shells) were designed to penetrate the armour of a thickly armoured enemy tank. HEAT warheads functioned by having the explosive charge melt a metal liner in the projectile to form a high-velocity superplastic jet but its effect is purely kinetic in nature. Contrary to a widespread misconception (possibly resulting from the acronym HEAT), the jet does not melt its way through armour. However, it is unlikely that the desired effect was frequently achieved on the battlefield. It is debatable whether the small amount of explosive contained in the shells was much more effective than the massive kinetic impact of a high velocity round.

As the war progressed the German approach was to seek improved anti-tank capability by mounting the largest possible calibre of main gun with the highest practicable velocity. The larger calibre effectively gave the tank a good high explosive firing capability and the kinetic energy from the high velocity gave it a deadly killing power against other tanks. The Panther tank of 1944 vintage was considered by many to be the ultimate combination of striking power, armour, and mobility. Five times as many Panthers were manufactured compared to the much more famous Tiger I and not surprisingly images of knocked out Panthers far outweigh the surviving photographs of their more famous cousins.

Despite the undoubted promise of machines like the Panther, German tank designers were still infatuated with the idea of ultra-heavy armour and massive hitting power over mobility. Late 1944 saw the completion of the super-heavy Panzer VIII – the

A Panther production line.

heaviest fully enclosed armoured fighting vehicle ever built. The Panzer VIII was initially to receive the name *Mammut* (Mammoth), although this was later changed to *Mäuschen* (Little Mouse), and finally to *Maus* (Mouse), which became the most common name for this tank. Weighing 188 metric tons, the Maus's main armament was the Krupp-designed 128 mm KwK 44 L/55 gun. The 128 mm gun was powerful enough to destroy all Allied armoured fighting vehicles then in service, some at ranges exceeding 3,500 metres. Five were ordered, but only two hulls and one turret were completed before the testing grounds were captured by the advancing Soviet forces. It seemed that the crazed minds of the Third Reich would never give up the quest to be the strongest and the biggest, whatever the cost, but as the humble Sherman and the T-34 had proved, sometimes quantity matters as much as quality.

Of the thousands of armoured fighting vehicles constructed by the Third Reich only a handful survive today. From a historical point of view it would be fascinating to have a much wider array of survivors but the lure of the scrap man's cash will always prevail over preserving redundant military hardware.

Although many German tanks were destroyed in combat with enemy tanks and anti-tank guns, the majority met their fate as a result of allied air attacks. As the war progressed a large proportion were blown up by their own crews either as a result of breakdowns and bogging down, or from a lack of fuel. However, what we do have to share is this – the surviving photographic record of the pivotal moments that saw these ingenious and hugely expensive fighting machines transformed from world threatening military hardware into redundant scrap metal.

May 1943 – A knocked out Panzer IV Ausf. G near the Italian city of Salerno.

1943 – An Allied DUKW passes a knocked out Tiger of the 504th Heavy Panzer Battalion in Sicily.

August 1943 – A Panzer III knocked out during the fierce street fighting in Centuripe, in Sicily.

1943 – A knocked out Tiger at Belpasso, Sicily.

September 1943 – A knocked out Panzer IV Ausf. G in Salerno.

1943 – The wreckage of a Sturmgeschütz III in Sicily.

August 1943 – A knocked out Sturmgeschütz III in the Sicilian commune of Sant'Agata di Militello.

September 1943 – GIs inspect the wreckage of a Panzerkampfwagen IV Ausf. G near Salerno.

18 September 1943 – A knocked out Panzer IV of the 16th Panzer Division at Paestum, Italy.

January 1944 – The wreckage of a Panther Ausf. G in France.

February 1944 – The wreckage of a Panzer IV in Italy.

14 February 1944 – A knocked out Panzerkampfwagen IV in Villagrande, Italy.

18 May 1944 – Two British soldiers inspect holes in the frontal armour of a Sturmgeschütz III (StuG III) assault gun knocked out near Aquino, a town approximately twelve kilometres northwest of Cassino.

Two knocked out Sturmgeschütz III Ausf. G assault guns in Italy.

A knocked out Tiger, destroyed during the battle for Lanuvio, Italy.

20 May 1944 – American 75mm self propelled gun and crew pass a knocked out German reconnaissance car near Itri, Italy.

23 May 1944 – GIs pose with the wreckage of a Marder III Ausf. H belonging to the 71$^{st}$ German Infantry Division in Italy.

25 May 1944 – The wreckage of a Panther Ausf. A near the Italian city of Latina.

28 May 1944 – An abandoned Tiger of the 508th Heavy Panzer Battalion in the streets of Cori.

28 May 1944 – A GI examines the wreckage of a Tiger belonging to the 508th Tank Battalion near Cori, Italy. In the background men of 3rd Infantry Division pass a second Tiger as they advance into the town.

British soldiers inspect a knocked out Panzerkampfwagen IV in Italy.

1944 – A knocked out Panzerkampfwagen IV near Rome.

4 June 1944 – Allied troops pass the burning wreckage of a Tiger on ther streets of Rome.

An Allied Sherman Tank passing a knocked out Panther during the advance on Arezzo.

1944 – A British soldier takes shelter from rain beneath tracks of a knocked out Tiger I abandoned by Germans in Italy.

7 June 1944 – A StuG III Ausf. G of Pz.Jg.Abt.709/709 Infanterie Division knocked out in Saint-Mere-Eglise by American M4 tanks of Coy. C 746th Tank Battalion supporting 82nd Airborne Division.

June 1944 – The wreckages of two Sturmgeschütz III's in Italy.

June 1944 – British troops advance past a knocked out Panther.

1944 – A knocked out Panther at St Gilles, France.

Four GIs pose for a photograph in front of a knocked out Panther in Normandy.

1944 – A Sturmgeschütz III destroyed by 9<sup>th</sup> Air Force aircraft in France. Note the open toolbox.

1944 – Knocked out Panthers south of Bretteville-l'Orgueilleuse in Normandy.

The wreckages of two Sd.Kfz 250 halftracks near the French town of Saint-Aubin-sur-Mer.

June 1944 – A Panther of the Panzer Lehr Division knocked out in Lower Normandy.

1944 – A knocked out Panther, destroyed by a British PIAT at Bretteville-l'Orgueilleuse, in Normandy.

June 1944 – The wreckages of a Tiger I of the 101st SS Heavy Panzer Battalion beside a Panzerkampfwagen IV of the Panzer Lehr Division in Villers-Bocage.

14 June 1944 – A knocked out Panther of Panzer Lehr Division. This vehicle was one of one of five knocked out in the village of Lingèvres by a single British Sherman Firefly of 4th/7th Dragoon Guards.

German wreckages in Normandy. The right frame (half track) resembles that of a Maultier (Opel).

1944 – A knocked out Panther in Normandy.

Two British soldiers crouch next to a downed Panzerkampfwagen III in Normandy.

19 June 1944 – Infantry of 2nd Battalion, Essex Regiment file past a knocked out Panther on a road near Tilly-sur-Seulles.

June 1944 – A GI inspects the wreckage of a Sd.Kfz. 138 Marder III Ausf. H at Terracina, Italy

20 June 1944 – A pair of knocked out Panthers lay to the side of a road on the outskirts of Lingevres.

June 1944 – A crippled Tiger of the 101st SS Heavy Panzer Battalion in the town of Villers-Bocage.

June 1944 – An American transport truck drives by the wreckage of a Panzer IV Ausf. H in Normandy.

27 June 1944 – A despatch rider passes a knocked out Sherman tank (in the foreground), and in the distance, a knocked out Panther near Fontenay-le-Pesnel.

June 1944 – An overturned Panther at Norrey-en-Bessin, France. The tank was probably up-ended during the Allied heavy bomber raid during the early stages of Operation Epsom.

June 1944 – A Loyd carrier and 6-pdr anti-tank gun of the Durham Light Infantry, 49th (West Riding) Division parked alongside a knocked out Panther.

1944 – French refugees pass a knocked out tank destroyer in Normandy.

1944 – A GI watches on as a knocked out Panther is dragged to the roadside in France.

27 June 1944 – A 6-pdr anti-tank gun crew of the Durham Light Infantry, 49th (West Riding) Division inspect a knocked out Panther during Operation Epsom.

27 June 1944 – Men of the Durham Light Infantry, 49<sup>th</sup> (West Riding) Division advance past a knocked out Panther during Operation Epsom.

A group of GIs inspect the wreckage of a Panther in Normandy.

A knocked out Panzer IV Ausf. H in Normandy.

30 June 1944 – A knocked out Panther near Rauray is passed by a British Sherman tank of 24th Lancers, 8th Armoured Brigade.

July 1944 – A Sherman tank in support of the 30th Infantry Division, passes by a pair of knocked out Panzerkampfwagen IV tanks neat Saint-Lô, during Operation Cobra.

Two GIs searching for mines pass by the wreckage of a Panther.

Summer 1944 – A variety of German armour knocked out and captured by the Allies in Normandy. A number of Panther tanks can be seen.

9 July 1944 – British paratroopers inspect a knocked out Panzerkampfwagen IV tank near Caen.

A pair of knocked out Panthers on the Marigny-Montrevil road in France.

1944 – A knocked out Panther Ausf. A on a roadside in France.

11 July 1944 – Knocked out Panthers of 1st company, 130th Panzer Regiment, Panzer Lehr in Normandy.

July 1944 – A disabled Panther belonging to the 116th Panzer Division, knocked out during fighting north of Saint-Pois.

16 July 1944 – A disabled Panther lies in a ditch on a road near Tourville.

1944 – Destroyed Sturmgeschütz III Ausf. G on the outskirs of Vire in Normandy.

18 July 1944 – American forces pass a knocked out Panzer IV near the Italian village of Pontedera.

20 July 1944 – A GI inspects a disabled Sturmgeschütz IV assault gun of the 17th SS Panzergrenadier Division *Götz von Berlichingen* at Periers, France.

Late July 1944 – The wreckages of a Panzer IV Ausf. H, together with two Sd Kfz 251 Ausf. D in Normandy. These vehicles belong to the 2nd SS Panzer Division *Das Reich*.

Late July 1944 – A pair of knocked out Panzer IV's of the Panzer Lehr Division in the ruins of Saint-Gilles, west of Saint-Lô in the so-called Roncey Pocket.

An American M4A1 Sherman passing a knocked out Panzerkampfwagen IV.

31 July 1944 – Destroyed Hummel *Clausewitz* and Sd.Kfz. 251 half-track of the 2nd SS Panzer Division *Das Reich* in Saint-Denis-le-Gast. These vehicles were knocked out by US 2nd Armored Division in the Roncey Pocket.

1 August 1944 – Carriers of the Queen's Regiment drive through a cornfield as a Panther tank burns in the background, during the advance towards Aunay-sur-Odon.

4 August 1944 – Royal Engineers search for mines near a knocked out Panther, near Villers Bocage.

August 1944 – GIs inspect a knocked out Panther near Autrey, France.

August 1944 – The wreckage of a Panzerkampfwagen IV Ausf. J (Sd.Kfz.161/2) of the 116th Panzer Division *Windhund* after the retreat from Falaise.

Allied soldiers examine the wreckage of a German self-propelled gun. This is most likely a *Brummbär*, a variant of the Panzer IV which was originally designed for use in the street fighting at Stalingrad.

Summer 1944 – A knocked out Panther belonging to the Panzer Lehr Division near Saint-Lô in Normandy.

5 August 1944 – Wrecked German Panzer IV Ausf. H, belonging to the Panzer Lehr Division, taken on St. Lo to Periers road.

1944 – Two GIs eat tinned food in front of a knocked out Panzerkampfwagen IV.

Bodies and wreckages litter the narrow lanes of the German route of escape in the Falaise pocket.

1944 – A team of GIs advance towards a Panther, knocked out by bazooka fire in Normandy.

August 1944 – A knocked out Panther and a dead German grenadier in the Falaise pocket.

A wrecked German half-track from an SS division lies on its side next to one of its fallen occupants. The American soldier is standing aboard a *Wespe*, one of the new breed of German self-propelled artillery which provided effective fire support for the Panzer divisions. They were, however, never available in adequate numbers; only 635 of these very useful vehicles were produced to satisfy the unceasing demands of both the Western and Eastern fronts.

1944 – An abandoned Jagdpanzer IV with a Pak 39 L/48 in France.

1944 – A column of GIs pass by the wreckage of a Panther in France.

A GI carefully approaches a knocked out Panther Ausf. A.

A GI approaches the burning wreckage of a German half-track.

GIs of the 3rd Armored Division examine a knocked out Sturmgeschütz III. A dead German crewman is slumped over gun barrel.

GIs celebrate with a captured German flag in front of a destroyed Panther. The group of infantrymen were left behind to "mop-up" in Chambois, France, the final German stronghold in the Falaise Gap.

US airmen check the results of their attacks on a Panther. The tank was neutralized along a hedge in Normandy.

Allied troops sift through the wreckage of a German supply column destroyed from the air as it retreated through the Falaise gap. In the foreground is the wreckage of a German half track. The German armies which took to the field in Normandy included over one million men, supported by over 1,500 tanks and some 3,500 guns. This vast assemblage needed over 20,000 vehicles and 20,000 horses. By the end of the campaign, the Germans had lost some 240,000 men killed and wounded, a further 200,000 as prisoners of war and practically all of the tanks, guns and vehicles.

An Allied Sherman passes American infantry standing amidst the wreckage of German armour. The numbered object to the right is the turret of a German tank, which has been completely blown off the chassis and turned upside down. The vehicle in the background is a Tiger.

August 1944 – An abandoned Tiger II of the 503rd Heavy Panzer Battalion on a roadside in Vimoutiers, France.

A vivid image of the destructive power wrought by Allied air forces in the confined spaces of the Normandy bocage.

A British Churchill passes the wreckage of a Panzer IV in a devastated French village. The object in the foreground is the turret of the tank which has been blown off by the force of the explosion.

August 1944 – GIs cautiously approach a burning Panther at Périers, France.

August 1944 – A column of German armour destroyed in Normandy during Operation Lüttich.

On a road lined with hedges, two GI's examine the wreckage of a Panther.

August 1944 – A knocked out Panzerkampfwagen IV.

16 August 1944 – A knocked out Panther Ausf. G photographed at an unspecified location in France.

20 August 1944 – A Sturmgeschütz III on its side in the river at Putanges, France.

1944 – A GI inspects a knocked out Panzer IV Ausf. H (numbered 725) of 7/Panzer-Regiment 26 in the Italian commune of Sezze.

21 August 1944 – A knocked out Sturmgeschütz III and soft-skin vehicles shot, damaged by Allied fighter-bombers in Normandy.

August 1944 – Destroyed half-track and two Panthers of the 2nd SS Panzer Division *Das Reich* after their failure against the Americans in Mortain, France.

1944 – Members of the 831st Engineer Aviation Battalion, Company A, who are building an aerodrome in the area, inspect a StuG III Ausf. G in the Vincennes area of Paris.

Schützenpanzerwagen (Drilling MG151s) anti-aircraft variant equipped with a triple-mount ("Drilling" in German means "triple") of MG151 autocannon; early version being MG151 15 mm cannon, later being MG151 20 mm Luftwaffe cannon (Falaise).

21 August 1944 – A knocked out Panther in the ruins of Argentan.

August 1944 – American forces pass knocked out German armour at Notre-Dame-de-Cenilly, France. An overturned Sdkfz. 251 is seen in the foreground, and behind that is the wreckage of a Panzer IV.

22 August 1944 – French civilians in a pony and trap pass a knocked out Panther tank in the Falaise-Argentan area.

1944 – A British soldier examines a knocked out Panzerkampfwagen IV in Italy.

A British soldier inspects a knocked out Panzerkampfwagen IV.

24 August 1944 – A knocked out Panzerkampfwagen IV tank in the Falaise pocket. A dead crew member lies on top of the deck.

August 1944 – A knocked out Hummel of the 12<sup>th</sup> SS Panzer Division *Hitlerjugend*.

25/26 August 1944 – A Tiger I knocked out on the riverside Rouen.

August 1944 – The aftermath of RAF attack on German transport equipment at Rouen.

25/26 August 1944 – Further evidence of the destruction at Rouen.

25 August 1944 – Three French boys gaze at a knocked out Panther in the Falaise pocket, Normandy.

7 September 1944 – A British soldier inspects a pair of Panzerkampfwagen IV tanks knocked out by 46th Division on the Gothic Line.

A Canadian tank M4A4 "Sherman" of the South Alberta Regiment is seen in the foreground and behind its lays a knocked out Panzer IV at Saint-Lambert-sur-Dive.

Military and civilian personnel gather around a knocked out Panther in Paris following the liberation of the city.

13 September 1944 – A knocked out Jagdpanther tank destroyer near Geel, a city located in the Belgian province of Antwerp. The Jagdpanther combined the very powerful 8.8 cm KwK 43 cannon of the Tiger II and the characteristically excellent armour and suspension of the Panther chassis.

September 1944, Marle, Aisne, Picardy – American GIs examine an abandoned Tiger I, left on the street by the retreating Germans as the Allies gained more ground in France. In the foreground are members of the French Resistance, identified by their distictive armbands.

GIs at rest in the rubble of Argentan. The Panther in the background was deployed by the 116th Panzer Division.

19 September 1944 – German prisoners photographed in front of a knocked out Panzerkampfwagen IV tank in the village of San Savino.

September 1944 – A GI stands on the hull of an abandoned Flakpanzer IV *Wirbelwind*. This self-propelled anti-aircraft gun was based on the Panzer IV, and was aimed at redressing Allied air superiority.

September 1944 – Brigadier General Elwood R. Quesada (General in Chief of the 9th Command and the 9th Tactical Air Command of the USAAF) inspects a knocked out Panzer IV Ausf. J in France.

14 October, 1944 – Panzerkampfwagen V (Panther) Ausf. A of 11. Panzer-Division, Ployart-et-Vaurseine, Champagne-Ardenne, France.

The carcass of a Sturmgeschütz M42 mit 75/18 850(i) near Aquino, Italy. The front suspension has been severly damaged and the rubber has been burnt form the surrounding roadwheels.

1944 – A knocked out Panzerkampfwagen IV Ausf. H in Normandy.

A Flakpanzer IV *Wirbelwind* knocked out during the Battle of the Bulge.

24 November 1944 – Infantry pass a knocked out Panzerkampfwagen IV on the road to Faenza, approximately 50 kilometres southeast of Bologna.

29 November 1944 – A Churchill tank rolls forward and in the distance a captured Panther deployed by the 4th Coldstream Guards. The action took place on the banks of the Maas.

A famous photograph of Panther 221 taken in La Gleize during the German attack in the Ardennes. It was one of fifteen Panthers left behind by *Kampfgruppe* Peiper.

A knocked out Pz.Kpfw. VI Ausf. B (King Tiger) numbered 104 of the 501st SS Heavy Tank Battalion. This tank was knocked out during the fighting in the Battle of the Bulge.

A GI sprints past a burning German half-track in La Glieze, Belgium, in 1944, during the German Ardennes offensive.

The wreckage of a Panzer IV in Normandy that has been stripped for parts.

GIs stands next to a knocked out Panther tank during the Battle of the Bulge.

1944 – Knocked out Tiger II in France.

1944 – A Tiger II knocked out during the Battle of the Bulge.

1944 – A GI near a knocked out German half-track Sd.Kfz.251/17 in the Ardennes.

A pair of GIs inspect the wreckage of a Panzerkampfwagen IV split in half by an American M10 tank destroyer during the Battle of the Bulge.

A Jagdpanzer destroyed during fighting with 3rd Armored Division in the Ardennes.

December 1944 – A captured Jagdpanther tank destroyer during the Ardennes Offensive.

December 1944 – An abandoned Panther near the village of Manhay.

A knocked out Tiger I of the 101st SS Heavy Panzer Battalion on the Western Front.

This shattered Tiger, its turret torn off by anti-tank fire, shows the ferocity of the American defence of their positions at Bastogne, the key town in the Ardennes.

The wreckages of a pair of Jagdpanthers during the Battle of Bulge.

The wreckage of a StuG 40 Ausf. G in Noville, Belgium.

18 December 1944 – A knocked out Tiger Ausf. B of the 501st SS Heavy Tank Battalion (part of *Kampfgruppe* Peiper) photographed on Rue Haut Rivage, Stavelot, Belgium.

17 December 1944 – Two Panthers that were knocked out by bazooka and rifle fire stand in a street in Krinkelt, Belgium. A dead German crew member lies across the back of the tank in the foreground.

December 1944 – A Panther Ausf. G knocked out on a road side in Holland.

GIs inspecting a damaged Sturmgeschütz III in Belgium.

1944 – The wreckage of a Sturmgeschütz III with added front armour in Charleroi, Belgium.

1944 – GIs inspect a knocked out Tiger II in Belgium.

Two GIs approach the smoldering wreckage of a Tiger during the Battle of the Bulge.

GIs passing the wreckage of a Tiger II (Nr. 223) in the area of La Gleize. The man in the centre of the photograph is armed with a German StG 44 assault rifle.

December 1944 – An American Dodge WC ambulance passes a knocked out Tiger II of the 501st Heavy Panzer Battalion, near La Gleize, Belgium.

A GI sits atop a knocked out Panther.

24-25 December 1944 – A knocked out Panther Ausf. G at La Gleize, Belgium.

24-25 December 1944 – A knocked out Tiger II of the 501st SS Heavy Panzer Battalion in La Gleize.

A knocked out Tiger II Ausf. B (King Tiger) in La Glieze.

29 December 1944 – Knocked out Panther tanks near Foy-Notre-Dame, Belgium.

A Jagdpanther destroyed by the Americans near Hargarten. Shell damage can be clearly seen on the glacis and the right track.

A Panzerkampfwagen V (Panther) Ausf. G burns fiercely after having been knocked out by an American Sherman tank on the road between Wirtzfeld and Krinkelt, in Belgium.

A GI of the 289th Infantry Regiment inspects a knocked out Panther of the 2nd SS Division *Das Reich* near Grandmènil, Belgium.

January 1945 – Captain James R. Lloyd, of the Ninth Air Force, poses next to a knocked out Sturmgeschütz III in the Ardennes.

January 1945 – The wreckage of a Panzerkampfwagen IV Ausf. J photographed in the Moselle-Saar salient, near the German-Luxembourg border.

6 January 1945 – Troops of the 327th Engineer Combat Battalion ready a Panzer IV for demolition to prevent the Germans from recovering the tank.

January 1945 – The wreckage of a Panther in Northern Luxembourg.

January 1945 – A knocked out Panzerbeobachtungswagen III covered in snow at Houffalize, Belgium.

Early 1945 – The wreckage of a Bergepanzerwagen III (Sd.Kfz 144) near Hosingen, Luxembourg.

1945 – A Panther Ausf. G and Panzer IV knocked out in Belgium.

January 1945 – A group of GIs inspect a pair of knocked out *Wirbelwinds* in the Ardennes.

1945 – A group of GIs stand beside a knocked out Panther Ausf. G *Befehlspanzer* in France. In the background is the wreckage of an American M32B1.

31 January 1945 – G.I.s from the 78th Infantry Division pass a pair of knocked out *Jagdpanzer 38*, or *Hetzer*, light tank destroyers in the village of Kesternich just inside the German border from Belgium.

31 January 1945 – A GI examines a knocked out German light tank in Ostheim, France. This tank was originally deployed in 1940 by the French 75th Division and was subsequently captured by the Wehrmacht. It was fielded as one of their *Beutepanzer* which were used to increase the number of German tanks in the field. These machines were manufactured by the French Hotchkiss factory and all instructions plates on it were in French.

9 March 1945 – A Panther knocked out by 9th Air Force fighter-bombers near the banks of the Rhine.

A member of the Eighth Air Force inspects a knocked Panther Ausf. G at Hosingen, Luxembourg.

1945 – A pair of GIs pose with the wreckage of a Panther Ausf. G in Belgium.

1945 – A knocked out Panther and PaK 40 in Stavelot, Belgium.

1945 – A group of GIs inspect a captured Sturmtiger, a heavy assault gun built on the Tiger I chassis and armed with a 380mm rocket-propelled round

18 March 1945 – A knocked out Jagdpanzer 38 (t) tank destroyer lies on the road to Saarlautern. The body of a crew member lies in the the foreground.

19 March 1945 – Four bazooka shells pierced the armour of this Tiger I. The tank, one track gone, was knocked out on the Western Front.

25 March 1945 – American forces pass a knocked out German vehicle (far right) at Kirchhellen.

29 March 1945 – A Panther Ausf. G knocked out during the capture of Haiger, Germany.

The Germans had clearly made a hasty attempt to camouflage this abandoned Panther Ausf. G.

A knocked out Tiger in Italy.

April 1945 – British soldiers inspect the wreckage of a Tiger found at Lugo, a town and commune in the northern Italian region of Emilia-Romagna.

10 April 1945 – A New Zealand tank passes a knocked out Tiger near the Senio river, Italy.

April 1945 – British soldiers pose alongside civilians with a knocked out StuG III in Zwolle, Holland.

16 April 1945 – British troops inspect a knocked out Panther Ausf. A of 1./Pz.Rgt.26 near Sesto Imolese, Italy. The vehicle has protective covers over the louvres on the rear plate and extra spaced armour on the turret roof.

16 April 1945 – The wreckages of two Panzerkampfwagen V Ausf. G (Panthers) at Sesto Imolese, just over the Sillaro River. Tank '434' in the foreground was commanded by *Leutnant* Drobnik and '424' in the background by *Oberleutnant* Hinz.